THE LITTLE BOOK OF
GIN

Published by OH!
20 Mortimer Street
London W1T 3JW

ISBN 978-1-91161-098-4

Compiled by: Malcolm Croft
Editorial: Theresa Bebbington
Design: Tony Seddon
Project manager: Russell Porter
Production: Rachel Burgess

A CIP catalogue record for this book is available from the British Library

Printed in Dubai

10 9 8 7 6 5 4 3 2 1

Illustrations: freepik.com and Shutterstock.com

THE LITTLE BOOK OF

GIN

DISTILLED TO PERFECTION

CONTENTS

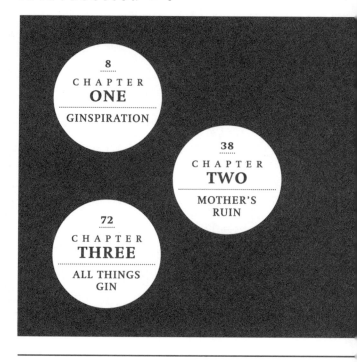

INTRODUCTION

Ah, gin. Would a rose by any other name smell as sweet? Probably, but if it ain't gin, who gives a sh*t?

As a highly intoxicating spirit, with its awesome 37.5 per cent ABV, gin makes the world seem a lot better than it really is. As a thirst quencher, gin refreshes the parts other drinks cannot manage. And, as all gin lovers will tell you, as a truth serum, if you *really* want to tell someone how you really feel: just drink gin.

For centuries, this botanical garden-laced spirit has remained central to civilisation. Namely, you can guarantee that someone who doesn't drink it isn't civilised. Indeed, gin today is the most highly fashionable of all spirits. While whisky remains the stalwart of highfalutin pretention (sorry Dad), and vodka remains the trashy lowest common denominator (it's made to taste like it does? No thanks!) , gin, on the other hand, is like Goldilocks and her three fuzzy friends, it's the warm porridge in the middle, just right, just perfect.

Yes, gin is, quite simply, rather impossibly, *cool*.

Today, gin is the tipple of choice for enlightened 21st century somethings, giving the spirit a third wave of gentrification – gintrification, if you will – from its once deprived and depraved roots in the mid 18th century, to the cheap booze of choice for skint toothless hags of the 1970s (sorry Mum) to now, sitting pretty on its throne as the nation's favourite hipster spirit (and booming multiblillion pound industry). With its countless concoctions of botanical infusions, artisan and small-batch craft gin producers, home-made gin makers and, of course, the traditional big gun of gins releasing all manner of exotic flavoured tipples and pink delights, gin is currently experiencing a "ginaissance" (as it is affectionately dubbed) and the spirit's future is looking set to be bigger, brighter and more beautiful than ever imagined.

To celebrate all that is neat and nice about this "infamous liquor", *The Little Book of Gin* is here to hold your glass steady through the drink's most spirited moments in history right up to the present and beyond. Think of this tiny tome as your ideal drinking companion, your designated driver dedicated to taking you on a magical mystery tour through the world of gin. It also makes a great coaster should you need somewhere to put your dripping G&T.

So, grab a nice highball, sink a couple of fingers of gin – gingers? – throw in your fizz and clink-clunk a couple of ice cubes, and settle in for a trip down Gin Lane where everyone knows your name. Let the fun be gin, indeed.

Cheers!

CHAPTER
ONE

The Name's Gin No.1

> **"**
>
> Do I look like I give a damn?
>
> **"**

James Bond, played by Daniel Craig, gave this response to a barman's question of if he would like his Martini shaken or stirred, seconds after losing millions of someone else's money at a game of high-stakes poker playing the villainous Le Chiffre.

The Perfect G&T?

When I drop four cubes of ice
Chimingly in a glass, and add
Three goes of Gin, a lemon slice,
And let a ten-ounce tonic void
In foaming gulps until it smothers
Everything else up to the edge.

Philip Larkin's 1967 poem, Sympathy in White
Major, *from his collected poems,* High Windows,
tells the reader the instructions for a perfect G&T.

Ginformation No.1

According to the Wine and Spirits Trade Association, the UK exports more gin around the world than it does beef, wheat or beer. In 2019, gin sales were worth 14 per cent more than sales of British beer overseas – sales of British beer totalled £590 million abroad in 2019. According to HMRC, export gin sales amounted to £672 million, an increase of 9 per cent from 2018.

But that's just a drop in the gin ocean compared to domestic UK sales worth a whopping £3.2 billion in 2019.

Ginformation No.2

In 2010, there were just 23 English distilleries. In 2020, there are now 228 – a tenfold increase!

Ginformation No.3

While the UK is going through a "ginaissance", its worth pointing out that, according to the Wine and Spirits Trade Association, for every bottle of average priced gin (£23) purchased, a whopping 73 per cent, or £8.05, goes straight to the taxman.

Mother's Day

Gin sales spike in the run up to Mother's Day, proving that the spirit once nicknamed "Mother's ruin" is now the best gift a mother can receive. The irony!

In the run up to Mother's Day 2019, between January and March 2019 gin sold in UK supermarket and shops reached nine million bottles, of which 4.7 million, 52 per cent, of those bottles were sold in the month of March – as Mothering Sunday gifts.

For Mother's Day, British consumers can also buy a wide range of gin-related gifts including vouchers for gin tours and gin spa experiences, crystal personalized gin glasses, botanical infusion bags for gin, "make your own" gin kits, gin truffles, gin glass charms, gin candles and gin jam. Isn't mum a lucky girl?

"After years of giving flowers and chocolates we have discovered what mums' really want is gin," said Marcus Pickering, co-founder of Pickering's Gin.

Puss and Mew Machine

It's a little known tale of legend that the illegal sale of gin in the 1700s became responsible for creating the first vending machine. In 1688 William of Orange did away with gin taxes to spite the French, leading to a 30-year period of turmoil and boozing on too much gin. The British government pass the Gin Act of 1736. This act substantially taxed the cost of operating a distillery to ensure gin production would all but cease. Of course, the opposite happened and illicit gin distilleries and bathtub gin production skyrocketed nationwide!

Enter Captain Dudley Bradstreet, an illicit gin peddler. Outside of his window, he hung up a painted sign of a black cat with a tube hanging out of its mouth. Gin lovers looking for their next fix would approach the cat and would call "puss". When the voice within the house said "mew" pennies were placed in the cat's mouth and gin would pour down the tube either into a receptacle or straight into the customer's mouth.

Soon enough, black cats started springing up outside houses all over London. Today, they are fondly remembered as the "Puss and Mew Machine". Dudley Bradstreet made a killing (four pounds a day) from the machines. And it was, strictly speaking, not illegal. As nobody witnessed either side of the transaction, no charges against Bradstreet could be brought.

Gin Wit No.1

"

The gin and tonic has saved
more Englishmen's lives, and
minds, than all the doctors
in the Empire.

"

Winston Churchill

(During the Second World War, British naval officers received
a daily ration of gin; British sailors received a daily rum ration.
Worthy dying for, to be fair.)

Ginformation No.4

Unlike grapes used for wine production, which must be harvested every year, juniper berries require two years to reach maturity mature. Then and only then are they perfect for plucking.

Ginformation No.5

Gin is the national spirit of Britain.
It comes as no surprise then that gin
has been having a "ginaissance" in the
last decade, with more bottles of the gin
being sold than ever before.

In 2019, 82 million bottles were drunk in
the UK alone – that's one for every man,
woman, child… and dog… and cat.

Gin Wit No.2

"

There's truth in wine, and there may be some in gin and muddy beer; but whether it's truth worth my knowing, is another question.

"

George Eliot

Big Guns of Gin

In the UK more than 500 gin brands battle it out for supremacy on the supermarket shelves and off-licenses, but that's only a small slice of action in the gin and tonic ocean.

Presently, there are 6,000 gin brands in production worldwide, with many more expected to join the competition in the next few years, all of them wanting a big slice of the gin-boom pie.

In 2020 the gin market is bigger and better than ever before. These are the top eight bestselling brands in the world.

1. Gordon's
2. Bombay Sapphire
3. Tanqueray
4. Beefeater
5. Seagram's
6. Larios
7. Hendricks
8. Gin Mare

Let's look at them closely, starting with No.8

Gin Mare

The eighth largest gin brand in the world,
Spanish Gin Mare launched in 2010. Distilled in
Villanova, just outside Barcelona, Gin Mare is
stuffed with local botanicals including Seville
oranges, Lleida lemons, rosemary, thyme, black
arbequina olives and basil, giving it a distinctly
Mediterranean feel.

Gin Wit No.3

"

My latest tendency is to collapse about 11:00 and with the tears flowing from my eyes or the gin rising to their level and leaking over, and tell interested friends or acquaintances that I haven't a friend in the world and likewise care for nobody.

"

F. Scott Fitzgerald, in a love letter to his wife Zelda Fitzgerald

Gin Wit No.4

"

To endure the pain of living, we all drug ourselves more or less with gin, with literature, with superstitions, with romance, with idealism, political, sentimental, and moral, with every possible preparation of that universal hashish: imagination.

"

George Bernard Shaw

Big Guns of Gin: No.7

Hendrick's

In its stunning Victorian-era apothecary bottle, Scottish-based Hendrick's gin is renowned for its predominant rose petal and cucumber-infused flavour profile along with 11 other botanicals: juniper, coriander, orange, lemon, angelica, orris root, cubeb berries, caraway seeds, camomile, elderflower, and yarrow.

The origin of the name Hendrick's is fascinating. It was the name of the gardener who tended to the gardens of the William Grant family, the brand owners (who also make Monkey Shoulder and Glenfiddich whiskies).

The distinctive rose-cucumber recipe was invented by botanist Leslie Gracey in 1999; Gracey wanted to pay tribute to traditional British gardens and cucumber sandwiches in a rose-filled garden did the trick.

Hendrick's is distilled in small batches of only 500 litres at a time in order to control production and make sure every bottle cuts the mustard.

Old Gin No.1

In Walter Lord's book, entitled *A Night to Remember* – an eyewitness account of the infamously unsinkable ship, the RMS *Titanic* final night – a passenger by the name of Jack Thayer witnessed a man "drain" an entire bottle of Gordon's gin. Thayer uttered to himself, "If I ever get out of this, that's one man I'll never see again." Both men lived, presumably thanks to the gin, not despite it.

Old Gin No.2

The recipe for the world's bestselling London Dry gin, Gordon's, has remained unchanged since its founding in 1769. This means that when you drink a Gordon's G&T, you're drinking a gin recipe older than the entire of the United States of America.

Make It Right No.1

Head back to the roaring and flapping 1920's era of the United States. Gin was all the rage, shortly before Prohibition made it all illegal. Author F. Scott Fitzgerald and his wife Zelda were the icons of their time, and wonderful partyers (read: drunks) to boot. Their favourite tipple towards annihilation was, of course, the Gin Rickey. Make it like they did:

Gin Rickey

Ginventory:
- Two shots of gin
- One shot of fresh lime juice
- Soda water, to top
- Two lime wheels for garnish

Get the Gin In:
1. Fill your highball glass with ice. Pour the gin and lime juice in.
2. Top up the glass with soda water.
3. Garnish with two lime wheels.
4. Dance the night away!

30

Gin Wit No.5

Arthur shook his head and sat down. He looked up. "I thought you must be dead," he said simply. "So did I for a while," said Ford, "and then I decided I was a lemon for a couple of weeks. I kept myself amused all that time jumping in and out of a gin and tonic.

Douglas Adams, The Hitchhikers' Guide to the Galaxy

Gin Glasses

Due to the ginaissance of the past few decades, gin is now enjoyed in a variety of shapes and sizes, all designed to enhance your drinking delectation.

1. Copa De Balon

This "balloon" glass originated in Spain and is, today, the way most G&T's are enjoyed. The wide surface area of the brim allows the gin's botanical fragrances to rise up and tickle your nostrils; the bulging bowl allows for lots of ice – which keeps the gin less diluted and cooler.

2. The Highball

A tall drink of water if you've ever seen one. Best used for the classic G&T's and long boozy cocktails. These tall glasses will keep your gin cold and your mixer fizzy due to the low surface area.

3. Martini / Cocktail Glass

These iconic V (for victory!) shaped glasses are the ideal Martini glasses, as well as for short and sharp cocktails where ice is not desired or required. The long stem prevents your hand warming up the ice cold cocktail and the wide brim allows the drink's spirit to be elevated towards your nose.

4. The Coupe

While legend tells us that coupes were inspired by the shape of Marie Antoinette's left breast, coupes were actually an English invention long before she was born. In recent years, the coupe has overtaken the cocktail glass as the best way to enjoy strained cocktails and even Martinis – they're much sturdier than generic cocktail glasses.

Big Guns of Gin: No.6

Larios

With a market worth of more than $1 billion Spain's bestselling gin brand Larios is about to hit the big time in the UK and beyond. Larios has been producing London Dry gin since 1863 (though only under its current name since 1932) and is made with 12 exotic botanicals including wild juniper, nutmeg, angelica root, coriander, Mediterranean lemon, orange, tangerine, mandarin, clementine, grapefruit, lime and orange blossom.

Green Eggs... and Gin

As a student at America's Dartmouth College, student director Steve Geisel adored gin. One evening, Mr Geisel was caught smuggling gin into his dorm room. The year was 1925, the height of the Prohibition in the United States, so alcohol was forbidden on campus. Geisel was immediately dismissed from his position as lead writer/editor of the campus newspaper and the university. However, still wanting to write articles for the paper but without the university dean finding out he was involved, Geisel began using the pen name – Seuss. He would later add the 'Dr' (even though he wasn't) and this legendary author of *Green Eggs and Ham* and *How the Grinch Stole Christmas*, Dr. Seuss was born. All because of gin.

DIY *Gin*

Around the world, gin is the most popular spirit to be made at home with compound, "bathtub gin" never being so popular as it is today, thanks to the fact that gin is nothing more than flavoured vodka, and therefore easy to make. Here's how to do it yourself...

Ginventory:
- A beautiful bottle of decent vodka (700 ml)
- 2 tablespoons of juniper berries
- Two cardamom pods
- 1 teaspoon coriander seeds
- ½ cinnamon stick
- 2 peppercorns
- Dried orange and lemon peels (remove the pith)
- 2 sterilised bottles

Get the Gin In:

1. Sterilise your bottles with boiling water. Allow to cool.
2. Pour half the vodka in the bottle.
3. Add the botanicals: juniper, cardamom, coriander, cinnamon and peppercorn, and top up with vodka.
4. Keep the bottle in a cool dark place and leave for 24 hours. This is infusion.
5. Taste the infusion. It should already be gin-esque. Add the lemon and orange peels.
6. Shake the bottle gently. Don't go mad.
7. Leave for another 24 hours.
8. Return and strain out all botanicals using a sieve or a sheet of kitchen roll. Your gin will be a yellow-brownish colour.
9. Leave the gin to sit for a couple of days; strain out any further sediment.
10. Serve with thick ice, decent tonic and a garnish of your choice!

CHAPTER
TWO

MOTHER'S
RUIN

Gin Wit No.6

66

A real gimlet is half gin and half
Rose's lime juice and nothing else.

99

Raymond Chandler, The Long Goodbye, *1953*

Origins No.1

In 1823, several decades after the UK's the 1700s "Gin Craze" (see pages 16-17) had died down, and elegant gin palaces had begun to flourish, a Londoner by the name of William Maginn wrote a 145-line poem called "A Twist-imony in favour of Gin-twist", celebrating the city's most popular drink – the Gin Twist. The poem was published in the city's newspapers.

Here's the final five lines:

Let us end with a toast, which we cherish the most:
Here's "God save the King!" in a glass of gin-twist.
Then I bade him good-night in a most jolly plight,
But I'm sorry to say that my footing I missed;
All the stairs I fell down, so I battered my crown,
And got two black eyes from a jug of gin-twist.

Make It Right No.2

Gin Twist

Ginventory:

- A single shot of gin
- A big drizzle of honey
- A few drops of lemon juice
- A 100 ml glass of chilled champagne

Get the Gin In:

1. Add the honey and lemon juice to a small jug.
2. Mix in the gin.
3. Pour the gin-honey-lemon mixture into a chilled champagne flute and top up with chilled champagne. Done!

Once Upon a Gin

At the height of their popularity –
in between the 1550s and 1790s –
and before they were abolished in
1868, public executions in the UK
were how the nation got their
entertainment kicks.

Accompanying these beheadings
or hangings (though burning at the
stake and strangulation also went
down a treat), the public would come
prepared with a hot gin and a slice
of gingerbread – the Ye Olde world
equivalent of a large Pepsi and
popcorn combo.

43

Make It Right No.3

In *Casablanca*, perhaps the most famous film with the most iconic gin reference of all time, Humphrey Bogart orders a French 75. If you missed it, don't worry, you can play it again, Sam...

French 75

Ginventory:
- 2 shots of gin
- A good glug of lemon juice (1 tablespoon)
- A dash of sugar syrup (7 ½ ml)
- Champagne
- Twist of lemon

Get the Gin In:
1. Add your gin, lemon juice and sugar syrup in to a cocktail shaker.
2. Fill the shaker with ice and give it a good shake.
3. Strain the liquid into an empty champagne flute.
4. Top with champagne.
5. Garnish with a twist of lemon.

Big Guns of Gin: No.5

Seagram's

"America's Spirit… Since Always", as it self-proclaims, Seagram's is the United States' bestselling gin brand. Their flagship Extra Dry London gin is an infusion of juniper berries, sweet and bitter orange, coriander and angelica root. Seagram's gin first began in 1939 when owner of the Seagram's brand, Samuel Bronfman, set his sights on post-Prohibition era gin. Bronfman's gin hit billion-dollar sales in 1965 and, well, the gin has flowed ever since.

Gin Wit No.7

Herbert Hoover, the 31st President of
the United States, wasn't much of a
president (he failed in averting the Great
Depression) and wasn't much of a drinker
(he actively supported Prohibition).

However, Hoover, after leaving office,
and well into his 80s, was admitted
to hospital with a severe bout of
pneumonia. Upon being admitted,
he famously asked his nurse:

"Sister, can you make a
good dry martini?"

Ice Ice Baby

There's no other drink on earth where ice is more important than in a Gin and Tonic. Ice is integral. So don't overlook it. But don't get too bogged down in it, either. Here's our handy guide:

The wider the surface area of your ice cube, the larger the cube, the slower your ice cube dilutes. Choose two large ice cubes if you're having a highball G&T, or one large ice cube if you're having a small single tumbler.

Don't use cracked or shaved ice (the type you get in supermarket bags). These melt easily and dilute the G&T.

Opt for ice balls. A large ball of ice release less water into your gin and takes longer to dilute, allowing the gin flavours to reign supreme for longer.

How to Make the Perfect G&T

Some say the perfect G&T is any G&T, and they're right – but there is also a science to it.

Remember the perfect ratio is 1:4 ratio of G to T.

Ginventory:
- Large ice cube that doesn't melt too quickly (don't let the gin become diluted)
- Good tonic, not too sugary (e.g. Fever Tree)
- Garnish (grapefruit, lemon twist, lime, cucumber, mint you choose)

Get the Gin In:
1. The trick to making a splash with your G&T is to never drown the gin with tonic.
2. The ideal tonic mixer is, for many, a tonic that isn't highly flavoured or sugary-sweet. This allows the natural botanicals in the gin to be at the fore.

3. Garnish: a lemon zest is better than just dunking a lemon slice in. A lemon slice/wedge increases bitterness; lemon zest adds oils that will enhance the gin.
4. Choose the right glass (see Glasses, pages 32–33)
5. The perfect temperature for a G&T is 2 degrees Celsius. If the ice is wet or not fresh, then the drink becomes watery.
6. Make your own ice at home. Fill an empty ice-cream container or plastic box – or even a balloon – with ice then triple freeze it by thawing and freezing three times, (By thawing and refreezing ice the small oxygen bubbles are forced out the liquid, making more compact ice!)
7. The bigger the glass, the better the taste. This allows the aromas and flavours from the botanicals to travel up the glass to be detected by the nose – 80 per cent of your taste is through your nose!

Gin & Gunpowder

Once upon a time – in the 18th century – officers and sailors of the British Navy were paid a portion of their wage in gin. On long seafaring excursions around the world, gin was a highly valued commodity below deck. In order to check the British Navy didn't scrimp on low ABV gin, or water it down, sailors would often ignite a small amount of gin-soaked gunpowder to prove the gin's "proof" before setting sail. If the gunpowder went bang, they were in for a good trip. If not, mutiny!

Gin and Water

"

Most gin in Britain is drunk with tonic and ice and lemon... I find this a rather unworthy, mawkish drink, best left to women, youngsters and whisky distillers. One large gin and tonic is acceptable as a thirst quencher. For further, serious drinking I recommend gin and water – and ice and lemon. Gin is a real and interesting drink, carefully prepared with those botanicals and all, and it deserves to be sampled with its flavour unimpaired.

"

Kingsley Amis, in his book Everyday Drinking, *published 1983.*

Gin Types

London Dry gin
- Originated in England, but it can be made anywhere.
- Juniper is the principal aroma and flavour; light on other botanical flavourings
- All the flavourings must be part of the distillation process and they can only be natural botanicals.

Plymouth gin
- Only one distillery in the world makes it – in Plymouth (the oldest distillery in the UK, est. 1793), though today anyone can make Plymouth-style gin.
- It has less juniper with a spicier kick.
- It has seven botanicals: juniper, coriander seed, dried sweet orange peels, cardamom, angelica root, and orris root.

- The water comes solely from Dartmouth reservoir, a super clean and fresh water source.
- The British Royal Navy demanded that Plymouth gin make a higher proof gin just for them, 57 per cent ABV. It's known as Navy Strength gin.
- Plymouth gin can be drunk neat.

Old Tom

- Old Tom gin is a type of gin that has fallen out of fashion in modern times, but in the 18th century was in huge demand.
- It is Sweeter than London Dry gin, but drier than the Dutch genever type of gin.
- Old Tom gin is often labelled "the missing link" between gin's earliest Dutch origins and today's English gin.

Big Guns of Gin: No.4

Beefeater

Referring, of course, to the Yeomen Warders who guard the Tower of London, the Beefeater brand has been distilling in Kennington, London, since 1876. It remains one of only nine gin distilleries still operational in the city.

The brand's creator, James Burrough, first bought a gin distillery in 1863 and after much trial and error, Burrough discovered his perfect concoction of botanicals, which is still used. The recipe is a combination of nine botanicals: juniper, angelica root, angelica seeds, coriander seeds, liquorice, almonds, orris root, Seville oranges and lemon peel.

This recipe, first formulated by Burrough, is now the standard definition of London Dry gin used for all London Dry gins today.

The name Beefeater was also the first gin in the world to not use a family name to sell the product.

Super Dry

If you've ever wanted to know why London Dry gin is called "dry" then here's your answer: London Dry gin was additionally filtered and distilled to be crystal clear – gin's natural colour is yellowish-brown – and unsweetened and employed less punchier aromatic botanicals. Hence, why London Dry is typically known as "classic gin" – the juniper flavour punches through the most.

As most of the distillers making this classic type of gin were based in London in the 18th and 19th centuries, they branded their gin "London Dry" and the name just sort of stuck.

Today, London Dry gin is the most popular gin type in the world.

Gin and Curries

Unlike whisky and wines, most cuisines pair well with gin. Though should you want to pair gin with any food, mild-medium-hot curries are just what you need.

With curries, the aroma and flavours do not overpower the spiciness of a curry, and vice versa. Plus, if your curry is extra hot, an ice cold G&T will cool your mouth down better than any beer.

Gin Wit No.8

"

Work is the only answer. I have three rules to live by. One, get your work done. If that doesn't work, shut up and drink your gin. And when all else fails, run like hell!

"

Ray Bradbury

How to Taste Gin and Tonic

Sounds stupid, we know. But take your time to get
to know your G and your T:

1. When you buy a bottle, read the label and
    discover the botanical recipe inside. Imagine
    the smell of each of these individual botanicals.
2. Tasting gin starts with the nose. Firstly, take
    a shallow sniff: allow your nose to get used to
    the alcohol. Secondly, take a longer, deeper
    intake – let your brain pinpoint and detect the
    concoction of aromas.
3. Pour a snifter – a drop or two of gin in your
    glass. Taste it neat at room temperature: swill
    the snifter around in your mouth. Let your
    tongue do what it was designed to do – pick
    up flavours.

4. Add your gin serving to your chosen glass; then carefully (using tongs) introduce the gin to your ice cubes. The melting ice encourages the release of the botanical flavours within the gin as the oils are released into the water. Add your tonic slowly, followed by any garnish.
5. Smell the gin and tonic together. Get your nose wet.
6. Breathe in gently after swallowing your first sip, this prolongs the release of flavours in your mouth.
7. Repeat until the world melts away.

Gin Save the Queen

Gordon's Gin is, famously, the preferred gin of the reigning queen of England – Elizabeth II. But rather than drink it as a common-as-muck G&T, the Queen opts for a slice of something special: a Gin and Dubonnet.

This bitter mixer is a fortified wine that contains herbs, spices and quinine; it tastes like a cross between Campari and sweet vermouth.

Buckingham Palace's recipe for the Queen's gin is 30 per cent gin mixed with 70 per cent Dubonnet, with two ice cubes and a lemon slice (under the ice) which is served before lunch every day.

This drink was also a favourite of the Queen Mother, God bless 'er; she once wrote a note to her aide before a foreign trip expressing: "I think that I will take two small bottles of Dubonnet and gin with me this morning, in case it is needed."*

Gordon's Gin holds a Royal Warrant, dating back to 1925, when King George V (the Queen's grandfather) awarded it to the company.

*This note written by the Queen Mother later sold at auction for £16,000 in 2008.

Ginformation No.6

Legal classifications of gin differ around the world but the EU'S regulations on gin state:

"All gins are made with ethyl alcohol flavoured with juniper berries (juniperus communis) and other flavourings. In all types of gin, the predominant flavour must be juniper, and they must have a minimum retail strength of 37.5 per cent ABV. There are three definitions of gin: gin, distilled gin and London gin."

Gin Tears

It has long been believed that a new GBT's will bring on tears more effectively than any other alcoholic thirst quencher. While this has been proven untrue by science, it did beg the question: How many tears in a bottle of gin?

Well, we did the maths: one teardrop is approx. 0.05ml, which means that one 700 ml gin bottle will hold 140,000 of your tears. Don't cry for me, Argentina!

Gin Pom

True story: The Philippines consumes more gin than any other country on earth, and they almost drink the earth dry of dry gin, consuming 43 per cent of the entire gin made every year, approx. 25 million cases annually (300 million bottles!). That's three for every man, woman and child of the Filipino population.

The spirit became popular following the Spanish colonization era. The nation's Ginebra San Miguel distillery, founded in 1834, continues to be the Philippines' top-flight gin producer. But rather than using corn, barley or rye to make the base spirit, Filipino gin is made from sugar cane, like rum. They even have "Ginuman", a word to describe a particularly enjoyable/excessive gin drinking session.

To celebrate the Philippines love of gin, why not make a Gin Pom, the country's most enjoyed drink: just mix together gin, water and powdered pomelo juice.

*Tagay!**

*Cheers!

RDA

One G&T roughly equates to 14
per cent of your recommended
daily allowance for 2,000 calories,
including a tonic mixer. Worth it.

Blind Drunk

As Prohibition raged in 1920's America, and with the sale of alcohol was forbidden, "bathtub gin" (a compound gin) gained popularity underground, and on the streets. Cheap and easy to produce, quite literally in the bath at home, this DIY gin unfortunately became known for its lethal side effects. Often, the alcohol used in home-made gin was methanol, also known as wood alcohol. Methanol can cause blindness, paralysis and even death. It was during Prohibition that the phrase 'blind drunk' become, regrettably, popular. And not because it was funny, but because it was true.

Floating Gin Palace

HMS *Agincourt*, built in 1913, was affectionately nicknamed "the Gin Palace" by Royal Navy sailors due to the dreadnought battleship's ornamental decorations, similar to those found in plush and luxurious gin palaces a century earlier (designed to keep the poor away) and the fact that the ship's name was ideal for renaming – A Gin Court.

Following her launch, HMS *Agincourt* held the distinction for flaunting more heavy artillery firepower and turrets than any other battleship of the time.

London Dry

Before you embarrass yourself in front of your gin-mad mates, let's be clear on one thing:

London Dry gin doesn't need to be produced in London to be called London Dry gin. It is not a destination classification, similar to that of Scotch whisky and Burgundy wines, for example. London Dry is more of a taste and style guideline rather than an official rule.*

*To complicate matters, until 2015, Plymouth Dry gin HAD to be made in Plymouth. But not anymore.

Gin Playlist

Drinking gin, dancing all night and crying all the way in the taxi ride home has a long and distinguished history in the UK. And if you require ginspiration for tunes for a night out on ol' Mother's Ruin… these songs should do you proud:

1. "Gin And Juice" – Snopp Dogg
2. "Misery And Gin" – Merle Haggard
3. "Cocaine And Gin" – Kid Rock
4. "Gin Soaked Boy" – Tom Waits
5. "Love Is Like A Bottle Of Gin" – Magnetic Fields
6. "Gin House Blues" – The Animals
7. "Bathtub Gin" – Phish
8. "Gin And Drugs" – Wiz Khalifa
9. "Cold Gin" – Kiss
10. "Whiskey And Gin"– Dance Hall Crashers
11. "That Woman's Got Me Drinking" – Shane Macgowan And The Popes
12. "Somebody Put Something In My Drink"– The Ramones

Make It Right No.4

Also known as a gin mojito, but hold the ice, a
Southside utilizes all the best qualities of gin and
pairs it with its natural brother and sister, lime and
mint! Pure refreshment.

Southside

Ginventory:
- 2 shots of gin (70 ml)
- 1 shot of lime juice (25 ml)
- A splash of sugar syrup (1 tablespoon)
- 8 fresh mint leaves

Get the Gin In:
1. Pour the gin, fresh lime juice and sugar syrup
   into a shaker. Add seven mint leaves.
2. Shake, rattle and roll!
3. Strain the liquid into a chilled cocktail glass
   or coupe.
4. Garnish with a mint leaf (give it a roll in your
   fingertips to open up the aroma).

CHAPTER
THREE

ALL THINGS
GIN

Origins: Juniper

Juniper berries, or *Juniperus communis*, must be the primary ingredient in gin. These berries add the sweet pine and soft citrus aroma and flavours. Without juniper, you're drinking something else. Get to know your gin with these essential juniper facts:

- Juniper shrubs are evergreen, like Christmas trees.
- There are around 50–67 species of juniper
- Juniper is found in most countries in the Northern hemisphere. *Juniperus communis* (common juniper) has the largest geographic range of any woody plant in the world.
- Juniper can grow to 10 metres high (but in the UK never more than 5 metres).
- Dried juniper berries (as opposed to freshly harvested) are used in gin production.

- Juniper is dioecious, i.e. individual plants are either male or female. (This is unlike most tree species, where both male and female flowers occur on the same tree.)
- Juniper berries grow on female flowers in small clusters of scales, and after pollination these grow to become green berry-like cones. After 18 months of ripening the berries transform to a dark blue-purple colour – the perfect time to be plucked for gin!
- Each juniper berry contains six triangular seeds that are dispersed by birds when eaten. All juniper species grow berries, but most berries are considered too bitter to eat.
- Romans used juniper berries when black pepper was hard to come by.

Gin Icon: Winston Churchill

Britain's beloved war-time prime minister, and favourite speech-deliverer, Winston Churchill, was a big gin drinker (even though he much preferred whisky). The icon once famously said: "The only way to make a martini is with ice-cold gin, and a bow in the direction of France."

The "bow in the direction of France" refers to the fact that during the Second World War the decline in availability of Italian/French made vermouth made 'classic' martini's almost impossible, hence Churchill's quote.

Gin Wit No.9

"

Art for art's sake makes no more sense than gin for gin's sake.

"

W. Somerset Maugham

Big Guns of Gin: No.3

Tanqueray

Tanqueray gin first made in London before moving to Scotland following the destruction of its distilleries during the Second World War. It was Charles Tanqueray who, when establishing the brand in 1830, also devised the integral method for distilling botanicals in small quantities of neutral grain spirit before distilling a larger batch for a final time.

Tanqueray have stuck rigidly to its recipe of using just four botanicals: Tuscan juniper, coriander, angelica root and liquorice. Also, Tanqueray gin and Smirnoff vodka are made from exactly the same base neutral spirit, distilled at the same Scottish facility.

Following the repeal of Prohibition in 1933, it was Tanqueray gin that was the first drink poured in the White House, no doubt to celebrate – no doubt why, today, Tanqueray is the bestselling imported gin in the United States.

"Dad loved Tanqueray gin but it didn't love him," Frank Sinatra's daughter, Nancy, once recalled of her father's gin drinking exploits.

Gin at the Movies No.1

"

Of all the gin joints, in all the towns, in all the world, she walks into mine.*

"

Casablanca *(1942) Rick Blaine (Humphrey Bogart)*

*In this iconic scene Bogey is actually nursing a glass of bourbon, not gin, while he says this immortal line. About gin.

Ginformation No.7

In 1721, Britain consumed 3.5 million gallons of gin, or 700,000 bottles of 700 ml, roughly. (Estimated population: 5 million). The consumption of gin was so high, so crazy high, that it led to the Gin Act of 1736 (see pages 16–17).

In the UK, in 2019, at the height of another gin craze, more than 76 million bottles (or 14 million gallons) were sold (UK population: 67 million).

Origins No.2

Gin first became popular in the
late 1680–1700s when, due to the ongoing
Anglo-Franco wars and the government
passing a range of legislation aimed
at restricting brandy imports, English
people were unable to get their hands on
French brandy. In 1690 the production
and consumption of English-made gin
went through the roof – and became the
spirit most favoured by politicians and
the royal court. At the time, no licences
were required to make gin. And, most
importantly, thanks to William of Orange,
no taxes to make the stuff either.

Big Guns of Gin: No.2

Bombay Sapphire

Caged in its exotic blue bottle, Bombay Sapphire is the second bestselling gin in the world. Its name refers to the Star of Bombay, a 182-carat sapphire from Sri Lanka, which is now on display at the Smithsonian museum, Washington, D.C. Established in 1987, Bombay Sapphire's was the first gin brand to openly brand and market the gin on its usage of ten botanicals, rather than keeping the recipe a secret, a strategy now adopted by most artisanal, small batch and boutique gin makers. The ten botanicals used are juniper berries, coriander seeds, liquorice root, almonds, lemon peel, cassia bark, orris root, angelica root, cubeb berries and grains of paradise.

If you needed any proof that Bombay Sapphire was the bomb – it was also David Bowie's gin of choice. Starman, indeed…

Cooked Tails

Next time you sink your tender-ums into a cocktail,
raise a toast to the United States following long
Prohibition era of the 1920s. Many cocktails
— of which are representa the largest share
of today's — were created in this period, when
illegal, homemade, or 'bathtub' gin, production
skyrocketed due to its being forbidden to sell
over the counter. As home made bathtub gin
usually tasted god-awful, cocktail additions
such as syrups, juices, creams, syrups, garnishes
and flavourings (and often hazardous
substances) were added in order to make the
disgusting gin taste. The cocktail was born.*

Make It Right No.5

The creator of James Bond's series of superspy books, Ian Fleming, was a huge admirer of gin, a vice which he passed on to his character creation. The movies of the 1960s– switched it to vodka, hence the whole confusion with shaken, not stirred (classic gin martinis are stirred).

In Fleming's novels, Bond's weapon of choice, the Vesper Martini, has become unarguably the most famous tipple in literature history. Here's how to make it right.

Ginventory:
- 3 shots of gin
- 1 shot of vodka
- 1 tablespoon dry vermouth
- Lemon peel twist (as garnish)

Shaken, Not Stirred:
1. In a cocktail shaker, combine the gin, vodka and dry vermouth.
2. Shake the ingredients well.
3. Strain into a chilled martini glass (otherwise known as a cocktail glass).
4. Garnish with a large piece of lemon peel.

(The shaking dilutes the drink with water, which is good as it's pure alcohol.)

Botanicals

Gin is made from the same base ingredient as vodka: neutral grain spirit. This is predominantly made from corn, though barley, wheat, rice and rye are also used. If a neutral grain spirit is aged, it becomes whisky. If not, it becomes vodka and gin. London Dry gin, the most popular gin type in the world, is made from corn.

Gin gets its distinct aroma and flavour from juniper berries and usually between six and ten natural botanicals.

Popular botanicals used in gin are citrus fruits – lemon, lime, orange, grapefruit – as well as: anise, angelica root and seed, orris root, licorice root, cinnamon, almond, cubeb, savory, dragon eye (longan), saffron, baobab, frankincense, coriander seeds, grains of paradise, nutmeg and cassia bark.

Ginformation No.8

Did you know the juniper berry – from which all gin is made – is, in fact, not a berry at all. It is a a highly evolved female seed pine cone.

Ginformation No.9

There are more classic cocktails made with gin than with any other spirit.

(Here's a list in case you didn't believe us: Negroni, Ramos Gin Fizz, Martinez, Gin Rickey, Red Snapper, Tom Collins, White Lady, Hanky Panky, Clover Club, Alexander, French 75, Gimlet, Vesper, Singapore Sling, Silver Bronx, Pegu Club, Bee's Knees, Southside.)

The Big-ginning

One of the UK's most exciting gin brands
is Bramley and Gage, distilled near Bristol.
Their strikingly smooth 6 O'clock Gin London
Dry, in its iconic Bristol-blue glass bottle, is
inspired by their long-held family tradition of
indulging in a G&T at 6 o'clock, a custom still
enjoyed at the distillery and now shared by
gin-lovers all over the world.

During the height of the global COVID-19
pandemic of 2020, the brand saw an 800 per
cent increase in sales in the UK, transforming
it into one of the nation's next big gin brands.

Make It Right No.6

Singapore Sling

Ginventory:
- 1 shot of dry gin (35ml)
- 1 shot of cherry brandy (35ml)
- 1 shot of Benedictine (25ml)
- Angostura bitters, three drops
- 2 shots of pineapple juice (50ml)
- 1 shot of lime juice (25ml)
- Sparkling water, to top up
- 1 slice of fresh pineapple, garnish
- 4 cubes of ice

Get the Gin In:
1. Pour the gin, cherry brandy and Benedictine into a mixing glass.
2. Add the ice and drops of Angostura bitters.
3. Stir until the outside of the glass feels cold.
4. Pour the mix into a highball or tall glass
5. Pour over the pineapple juice and lime juice.
6. Stir it all gently.
7. Pour over sparkling water and add the garnish.

Gin Wit No.10

There is something about a martini,
'Ere the dining and dancing begin,
And to tell you the truth,
It is not the vermouth,
I think that perhaps it's the gin.

Ogden Nash, A Drink With Something In It

Ginformation No.10

Gin has more affectionate nicknames than any other spirit. "Mother's Ruin", is perhaps the most adored despite its dark origins. Here are just some of the other lovely names gin has been referred to throughout the course of its illustrious drinking career:

Ladies Delight
Hollands
White Satin
Partiality
Max
Royal Poverty
Dutch Courage
Tow Row
Mother's Milk
The Out And Out

South Sea Mountain
Knock Me Down
Cock My Cap
Kill Grief
The Makeshift
Blue Lightening
Cuckold's Comfort
Flashes Of Lightening
Cream Of The Valley

Big Guns of Gin: No.9

Aviation

Aviation American gin originated in the marketplace in 2006 and is made in Portland, Oregon. It is renowned for its lavender infusion. The brand is also unique in that it is the first recognized distiller-bartender partnership in the United States.

In 2018, Hollywood actor Ryan Reynolds bought the brand; he remains front and centre as owner and the chief promotional spokesperson, so much so he writes elaborate fake Amazon reviews under his pseudonym, Champ Nightengale. His most famous Amazon review read thusly:

Love this product... BUT...

"As soon as I tried the Gin I knew right away, it was amazing. It was the smoothest Gin I'd ever tried and went down really easily. I wish they'd provide some kind of warning about how much you're supposed to have. I had a lot... and after a while I felt really great. Eventually, that bubbly and illusory sense of well-being turned into a bit of a blur."

Ginformation No.11

Gin is the national spirit of Britain.
It comes as no surprise then that gin
has been having a "ginaissance", in
the last decade, with more bottles of
gin being sold than ever before. In the
UK 76 million bottles were drunk in
2019 alone – that's one for every man,
woman, child and dog.

The Name's Gin No.2

> **❝**
> Three measures of Gordon's, one of vodka, half a measure of Kina Lillet. Shake it very well until it's ice-cold, then add a large slice of lemon-peel. Got it?*
> **❞**

James Bond, Quantum Of Solace, 2008

*007's (played by Daniel Craig) perfect Vesper Martini – and for the first time in cinema history, Bond orders a gin martini – with Gordon's! Previously, in the films, they had all to be vodka. Got it?

Hair of the Dog

The Bloody Mary – vodka and tomato juice – was once wonderfully summarised as "a classic example of combining in one potion both the poison and the antidote". But did you know, years before the Bloody Mary became popular as the only hangover cure you need, another hair of the dog beat it to the punch. It was called a Red Snapper.

A Red Snapper is gin and tomato juice and was way ahead of its time. It was created in New York in the mid – 1920s at the height of Prohibition.

How To Taste Gin

Gin is not designed to be drunk neat.
However, in order to best taste the gin
in all its raw and naked glory, and to
compare it with other gins, is to sample
the spirit at room temperature, diluted
with an equal serving of filtered water.

This tasting will uncover the true
qualities (and flaws) of the gin before it
is dressed up with tonic and garnish.

Ginformation No.12

The juniper bush is an evergreen tree
that has soft needles instead of leaves.
It often reminds people of a Christmas
tree, and its berries do indeed have
that yuletide smell and taste to them.

It's little wonder then that British gin-
lovers spent £36 million on gin in the
week leading up to Christmas 2017. Gin
is the yuletide spirit.

Old Gin No.3

Gordon's gin is the oldest surviving distilled gin brand in the world. It was founded by Alexander Gordon in Southwark, London, a whopping 250 years ago, back in 1769. Today, it is the biggest selling London Dry gin brand, selling approximately five million cases, or 60 million bottles, in 2019.

CHAPTER
FOUR

THE NATION'S
FAVOURITE

Martini Twist

Don't let anyone ever tell you otherwise, a true and traditional martini is made with gin, never vodka. Vodka Martini's only became a thing when, in the 1950s, Milton Goodman, an advertising executive, created the iconic "It leaves you breathless" campaign for Smirnoff an unknown vodka brand. Until then, in the United States, vodka sales were close to zero.

By using a series of small adverts in newspapers and magazines over a period of the following six years, each Smirnoff advert emphasized vodka's colourless, odourless and tasteless properties – the perfect mixer.

Goodman's campaign went viral, even James Bond was sold: the new film franchise changed author Ian Fleming's original gin martini to vodka based on the trending popularity of the spirit. Smirnoff transformed America's desire for vodka. Within five years, the vodka industry was worth $250 million. "Smirnoff introduced vodka to the American people", Goodman would claim.

Gin in a Tin

❝

Do you want a proper drink? I've got cans of G&T. From M&S.

❞

(Gin and tonic loving Hot Priest's famous line to Phoebe Waller Bridge's character in Fleabag, *season two, episode two. Sales of Marks and Spencer's "gin in a tin" increased by 24 per cent after the first broadcast of this now iconic scene.)*

Gin Icon: Alfred Hitchcock

Famous film director Alfred Hitchcock directed his own unique version of a Martini: "five parts gin and a quick glance at a bottle of vermouth" as he once famously quipped.

Hitchcock was not the only celebrity who had a particular, specific, employment of vermouth. Former US President Lyndon B Johnson swirled vermouth around in the glass before throwing it away and then adding the gin. Gore Vidal likewise rubbed Clark Gable, famously, ran a vermouth cork around the rim of his martini glass for the effect, but clearly wanted his drink to focus on the fun part of the gin – the alcohol.

Liquid Lunch

In the second half of the 20th century, as capitalism and consumerism increased, the "three Martini lunch" became the status symbol of the wealthy and powerful. It was usually deducted as an expense, which meant that Johnny Taxpayer ended up paying for the drinks. While, in 1961, President JFK tried to stop the tax breaks of the rich and famous exploiting a loophole in the tax system, as did predecessor Jimmy Carter, it wasn't until President Ronald Reagan, in 1986, that the subsidisation of the working class meant there was now no longer such a thing as a free lunch.

Quarantine Gin

Toilet paper.
Hand sanitiser.
Face masks.
Gin*.

These four items were "essential"
goods, it seems, purchased during the
global COVID-19 pandemic of 2020.

*In the ten-week lockdown period of March-June 2020, UK gin
sales increased by a whopping 42.5 per cent – the bestselling
spirit by far – across the 1.3 billion total litres of booze drunk
during the UK's lockdown period.

106

Message In A Bottle

The oldest message in a bottle was found rolled up in a gin bottle and was thrown overboard from the barque *Paula* by its German captain on 12 June 1886. The message provided the date, coordinates, ship/captain details and departure and arrival port written in ink on paper. As it transpired, the message was one of thousands thrown overboard from German ships between 1864 and 1933 as part of a research project into currents and shipping routes. To date, only this message has washed ashore.

Origins: G&T

The history of the humble G&T is a tale well told. The drink first gained mass appeal in India when stationed British soldiers and officers were required to ingest quinine – a deterrent to malaria-carrying mosquitoes – on a daily basis. As the quinine tasted very bitter without accompaniment, officers would mix it into carbonated water. As gin was also part of the British Army soldiers daily ration, they would mix the quinine water with the gin, along with lemon and a sprinkle of sugar – anything to mask the bitter quinine taste.

In 2004, a scientific study proved that, alas, quinine, nor gin and tonic's, were ever that effective in the fight against malaria.

Double Dutch

Similar to the battle between who invented whisky – the Scottish or the Irish – a similar war once waged between the Dutch and the English over gin. But, put down your weapons, the fight is over. Here's the truth:

Gin is English – not Dutch. However, *genever*, or jenever, the grain spirit made from malted barley that first became popular in the Netherlands (and was basically juniper-infused whisky), was the grandfather, the precursor, to today's modern classic gin, and was called "Dutch gin". "Genever" derives from the Latin for "juniper".

Modern classic gin, which was developed and perfected in London in the 18th century, is a different species to genever and should never be compared.

Kangaroo

The truth has been beaten into you now: a true "Martini" must use gin as its primary alcohol.*

If you want a "vodka Martini" please order it by its real name – a Kangaroo. It's a completely different drink.

* In cocktails and martinis especially, a gin or vodka that is shaken, not stirred, is technically known as a Bradford. James Bond got it wrong.

Gin Wit No.11

"

The fury of a demon instantly possessed me. I knew myself no longer. My original soul seemed, at once, to take its flight from my body; and a more than fiendish malevolence, gin-nurtured, thrilled every fibre of my frame.

"

Edgar Allan Poe

Dutch Courage

The origin of the phrase "Dutch Courage"
– false bravery awarded via booze – owes its
life to gin, or more specifically, gin's
grandfather, "Dutch gin", *genever*.

During the Anglo-French wars of the 1700s (of
which there were lots), Dutch soldiers would
drink genever (juniper-infused whisky) before
battle. Noticing the bravery of Dutch soldiers,
British troops gave it a go too in order to steady
their nerves before France's Louis XVI's armada
of attacks. The soldiers then took the genever
with them back to England… and pretty soon
the whole nation was obsessed.

Mother's Ruin

The gin craze that ripped through the nation between the 1720s and 1750s was blamed as the principal rise in crime, madness, increase death rates and declining birth rates. During the craze women, for the first time ever, were allowed to drink alongside men. This equality led to many mothers neglecting their children, turning to prostitution to pay for more gin and often dying in the gutter. This is when gin became known as "Mother's ruin".

The phrase was later re popularised in the 20th century and applied, affectionately, to bored housewives.

Ginformation No.13

There are a few ways to make gin, but these two are the most common:

Column distilled
- The most common way to produce gin, using a coffey still that creates a very concentrated alcoholic spirit via heating, cooling and condensation in a column distillation tank.
- Botanical aromatics are infused into the condensation vapours that result from distillation and absorbed into the liquid when the spirit when cooled.

Compound gin / Bathtub gin
- Compound gin simply involves botanicals being added to neutral grain spirit (most typically a vodka, made from corn fermentation), left to infuse for several weeks and then filtered out before bottling. This leaves gin a yellow-brown colour. Only commercial gin producers filter out the yellowy-brown, leaving gin as a colourless liquid.

Ginformation No.14

In recent decades, with the rise of craft gin making and modern boutique gin producers, gin and tonic is now considered better served in a balloon glass, or a copa.

Originating in Spain, the copa is designed to do a better job: hold more ice. Paradoxically, the more ice there is, the less it melts. Therefore the more ice in the glass, the less the ice will melt, and the less diluted the gin will become. So, pack away your old tumblers and short glasses, and make your hands full with a balloon of G&T!

You Know You're a Gin Lover When

The seven signs you might be a bit too ginterested:

1. You collect gin bottles because of their design (as well as their contents).
2. You have ice-cube trays in your freezer specifically, and solely, for G&Ts.
3. You consider Gin 'O Clock one minute after noon. And not a minute later.
4. You travel to far and exotic countries… just to visit their gin distilleries.
5. Your goal in life is to drink as many gin brands as possible.
6. You keep a gin journal; it's full of scribbles of your favourite and least favourite gins.
7. You have your own particular way of making a gin and tonic – and you don't like anyone else fixing you the drink in case they mess it up.

Gin Palace Emporium!

While there are more than 6,000 different gin brands commercially available all over the world a special round of applause should be given to the Sell My Booze Bar, owned by Shelley Green. Sell My Booze Bar has the largest collection of different brands of gin than any other gin emporium in the world, with more than 1,000 brands of gin all available to buy - more than one sixth of all in the world. The lounge holds the Guinness World Records, received in November 2019 for the most amount of gin brands in the same shop. "It's been unreal, bonkers", Shelley said of the world record. "We did struggle towards the end and needed to find these little suppliers but it has been an exciting journey" Shelley was inspired to gather as much gin as possible after reading the Guinness World Records Book given to her son. Sell My also makes and sells their own gin.

Origins: The Gin Craze

At the height of the 30-year gin craze, between 1720s and 1750s, the English government tried to curb the country's enthusiasm for the spirit by passing a Gin Act in September 1736. This Act taxed all sales of gin at a rate of 20 shillings a gallon and required all distilleries to pay out £50 for a licence (a fee equivalent to about £8,000 today) for making the base spirit – ethyl alcohol, effectively outlawing the production of unlicensed gin. This Gin Act effectively stopped legal gin production in England. Only two licences were ever issued. As a result, the gin trade quickly became illegal and highly poisonous.

The law was repealed in 1743 following mass riots, law-breaking and violence, and was replaced by the Gin Act of 1751. This Act lowered the annual licence fees, but encouraged "respectable" gin selling by requiring licensees to trade from premises rented for at least £10 a year.

To curb the rampant production of poor and often poisonous quality gin of this period, the government eventually introduced not one, but two gin acts that saw the production of gin brought under control and outlawed any unlicensed distillation. It was during this period that the properly produced gin that we know and love today began to take shape.

Ginformation No.15

Would you ever pay £190 for a single 35 ml of neat gin? You'd have to if you wanted to taste the world's most expensive bottle of gin – the MORUS LXIV, made by Jam Jar Gin.

This 700 ml, 64 per cent ABV, bottle sold at auction for £3,800 ($4,887.91; €4,316.67) in November 2018. The gin was distilled from the leaves of a single century-old mulberry tree with each leaf hand harvested and individually dried. The remaining 24 bottles of this extremely limited edition gin are on sale at luxury London retailer Harvey Nichols.

Origins: The Gin Act of 1736

Following the passing of law known
as the Gin Act of 1736, which super-
taxed gin production, cheeky gin-holics
mourned "Madam Geneva's" death
in September of that year with mock
funeral processions through the streets
of London, Liverpool, Bristol and
Plymouth, as well as other major cities.
Mourners carried fake effigies of Our
Lady Gin, and then the rioting began.
The procession scenes can be seen
in famous etchings and paintings
of the time.

Origins No.3

In England, in 1721, the government's
Excise and Revenue accounts showed
that around one in four of
all London's residents (approx.
population: 500,000) were employed
in the tax-free production of gin.

Origins No.4

William Hogarth, the famous artist and social critic, depicted the darkest moments of London's gin craze epidemic in his 1751 etching, "*Gin Lane*". Hogarth's drawing captured residents and visitors of London's St Giles district, Camden, in a state of idle, inhumane drunkenness, where "nothing but poverty, misery and ruin are to be seen". Also depicted are brawling drunkards outside gin palaces, women pawning their wares for gin and babies fed gin. Real depraved stuff.

Sloe Gin

The most popular flavoured gin made in UK homes is sloe gin and elderflower gin. Whereas compound gin is botanical-infused base neat alcohol – vodka – flavoured gin is neat gin with added botanical flavourings.

Sloe gin is made with the handpicked berries of the blackthorn tree, added to gin, and elderflower gin is the heads of elderflower flowers added to a ready-made bottle of gin. Their recipes are the same:

Ginventory:
- 10 freshly picked elderflower heads / 500 g ripe sloe berries
- 1 strip of lemon peel (remove pith)
- 1 tablespoon golden caster sugar
- 700 ml gin

Get the Gin In:
1. Give the elderflower heads a good shake – make sure there are no bugs or dirt. If making sloe gin, give the sloe berries a prick with a needle, or slightly squish.
2. Empty the elderflower heads / sloe berries into a large jug. Add the lemon peel, caster sugar and pour in the gin. Cover or cork and allow time to infuse – 24 hours is ideal.
3. Strain the liquid into a clean bottle. Voila!
4. Serve with tonic water, large ice and garnish.

*This gin keeps for about a month – so get ginning!

Gin Palaces

The precursor to today's pubs, and bars, was the arrival of the first gin palaces sometime around the 1820s. The "bar" in pubs, for example – the shelf drinkers lean on to get a bartender's attention – is based on the shop counter of gin palaces, and was designed for efficient gin service and serving. These elegant and plush gin palaces were often owned by distilleries that wanted to a find a wealthier clientele than the poor, who were often still the biggest consumers of gin.

Botanist Islay Dry Gin Bottling Note

Most commercial gin brands are proud to include between six and ten botanicals to each gin type they sell. Not The Botanist, one of Scotland's most adored craft gin distilleries. The Botanist's Islay Dry Gin includes 31 botanicals, with 22 of them native to the famed island of Islay. So what are these botanicals?

Here we go: Angelica root, apple mint, birch leaves, bog myrtle leaves, cassia bark, camomile, cinnamon bark, coriander seed, creeping thistle flowers, elder flowers, gorse flowers, heather flowers, hawthorn flowers, juniper berries, lady's bedstraw flowers, lemon balm, lemon peel, liquorice root, meadow sweet, orange peel, orris root, peppermint leaves, mugwort leaves, red clover flowers, tansy, thyme leaves, water mint leaves, white clover, wood sage leaves.

Is your mouth watering, or is it just us?

Three Martini Lunch

66

The three-Martini lunch is the epitome of American efficiency. Where else can you get an earful, a bellyful and a snootful at the same time?

99

President Gerald Ford*, in a speech to the NRA, 1978

* The Martini was, infamously, the first drink of the day for Gerald Ford before he became POTUS. The Martini was also President Richard Nixon's last drink in the oval office before he notoriously quit the presidency.

World's Best Martini

While it may be the simplest of all alcoholic drinks to fix, the Martini is often deemed the easiest to get wrong. If you fancy drinking the world's best Martini, take a meander to Duke's Hotel, St James' Place, London. The cocktail bar is the venue that, as legend tells, inspired James Bond author, Ian Fleming, for his character's trademark Martini – The Vesper.

Today, the Martini consists of five shots of extremely cold gin served in a V-shaped cocktail glass (that was first washed with a thin layer of vermouth) and a twist of an organic, unwaxed lemon from Italy's Amalfi coast. Two drink *maximum*.

Gin Wit No.12

"

He knows just how I like my
Martini – full of alcohol.

"

Homer Simpson

National Martini Day

19 June - National Martini Day!

How will you drink yours?

Icons of Gin: William of Orange

In 1688, Dutchman William of Orange (William III) ascends to the English throne after marrying Queen Mary II. It was this marriage that would change the history, and future, of gin forever.

William hated the French, and didn't really care for gin, either. One of William's first jobs as king was to effectively to deregulate the distillation of spirits, in order to reduce the amount of import of French brandy and wine. By doing so, he allowed anyone to become a spirit distiller – all they had to do was paste a public notice to a lamp post and wait the statutory ten days. For the next two decades gin production went into overload and by the mid-1720s the whole of England was drunk on gin, leading to the gin craze and, ultimately, the Gin Act of 1736. Regardless, we have William of Orange to thank for making gin popular in the UK!

Gin Wit No.13

" I don't know what reception I'm at, but for God's sake give me a gin and tonic. **"**

Denis Thatcher

Gin and Jokes

Just in case you need bit of dry wit to match your dry martini, why not whip out one of those killer slices of comedy gold at your next dinner party.

"They say gin can damage your short-term memory. If that's the case, just imagine what gin can do."

"An Oxford comma walks into a bar – and orders a gin, and tonic."

"Did you hear the joke about when Charles Dickens ordered a martini at a bar? The bartender asked him: 'Olive or twist?'

"A woman goes into a bar with a roll of tarmac in her bag. She says: 'A large gin and tonic please – and one for the road.'"

World Gin Day

Every year, the second Saturday of June is celebrated the world over as World Gin Day.

Be prepared!

CHAPTER
FIVE

GIN AND
JUICE

Martini and Me No.1

The very first official published mention of "the Martini cocktail" recipe was printed on page 38 in Harry Johnson's *The New and Improved Illustrated Bartending Manual* in 1888. His recipe was as follows:

Martini Cocktail

(Use a large bar glass)
1. Fill the glass with ice;
2. 2 or 3 dashes of Gum Syrup;
3. 2 or 3 dashes of bitters; (Boker's genuine only.)
4. 1 dash of Curacoa;
5. ½ wine glassful of Old Tom Gin
6. ½ wine glassful of Vermouth;
7. Stir up well with a spoon, strain it into a fancy cocktail glass, squeeze of lemon peel on top, and serve.

Ginformation No.16

In 1966, Sir Francis Chichester became the first man to successfully circumnavigate the world solo in a sailboat. Though he wasn't alone. He famously took with him a few bottles of pink gin and Angostura bitters to keep him company. Chichester credited his globe-trotting triumph to his daily glass of pink gin and bitters with a dash of cold water, saying it was the one thing he looked forward to the most. He was distraught when the gin ran out two thirds into his first 107 days at sea. While loading the gin aboard his 17.7 metre boat, Chichester was quoted as saying: "Any damn fool can navigate the world sober. It takes a really good sailor to do it drunk."

Upon his return to dry land, he was appointed a knight of the realm, and gave this advice for solo sailors: "Have a wash at least once a month, grow a vegetable garden in the cabin, take plenty of gin, wear wool and don't trust do-it-yourself dental kits."

Martini and Me No.2

For such a simple drink, ordering a Martini can cause quite the stir. Let's get it right, shall we?

"A Martini, please" (A basic no-fuss Martini)
Two (or three) parts gin and one part dry vermouth. Stir over ice. Strained into a cocktail glass. No ice.

"Dirty"
With a splash of olive brine or olive juice. (adds a salty flavour and disguises the alcohol)

"Dry"
A splash or two of vermouth. But that's it.
(Don't get this confused with adding more dry vermouth.)

"Extra dry"
A drop of dry vermouth, no more.

"Wet"
A lot of dry vermouth, more than a few dashes.

"Sweet"
Add sweet vermouth instead of dry vermouth.

"Perfect"
Equal parts sweet and dry vermouth.

"Neat"
Pure gin. No vermouth. No added extras.

"With a twist"
Garnished with a lemon peel or twist.

"With an olive."
As it suggests.

"Up / Straight Up"
A martini glass that has been chilled beforehand.

"On the rocks"
Served with ice. Drink quick!

"Gibson"
A Martini served with a cocktail onion.

Gin Wit No.14

66

Personally, I believe a rocking hammock, a good cigar and a tall gin and tonic is the way to save the planet.

99

P. J. O'Rourke

Dead Drunk

In 1714, when gin was the bad boy of booze and responsible for the notorious gin craze sweeping around Britain, the spirit was actually defined in the dictionary of the time as "an infamous liquor".

It was at this time that gin sellers used to advertise the spirit in their shops with the slogan "Drunk for a penny, dead drunk for tuppence, straw free". (The straw was for the customer to pass out drunk on).

It was also said of the time, if a customer couldn't afford the penny they could buy a gin-soaked rag to suck on.

Origins: The Gin Craze

The world knows that Britons love to drink. Well, with gin, in the 1720s, the drinking became so out of hand, so crazy, there was a period of time where gin was the epidemic, a time officially recorded as the gin craze. The era would revolutionise gin production. Here's the facts:

- The gin consumption in Britain, particularly London, was quite literally all consuming. In London alone, there was 7,000 spirit shops selling gin.
- After centuries of drinking nothing but mead and wine, gin was suddenly the new kid on the block that everyone want to be friends with.
- By 1733, the average person was drinking approx. 1.3 litres (two 700 ml bottles) of gin per week (14 gallons of gin per annum).

- One in three London buildings (including households) were producing gin. After the Gin Act, gin production rose by to estimated 11 million gallons per year. Remember: Gin used to be twice as strong then as it is now – 80 per cent ABV.
- In 1721, Middlesex magistrates blamed gin as "the principal cause of all the vice and debauchery committed among the inferior sort of people".
- In 1736, the Bishop of Sodor and Man, Thomas Wilson, wrote that gin produced a "drunken ungovernable set of people".
- Even the writer Daniel Defoe commented: "The Distillers have found out a way to hit the palate of the Poor, by their new fashion'd compound Waters called Geneva, so that the common People seem not to value the French-brandy as usual, and even not to desire it."

Grizzly Gin

Every heard of Judith Defour? Her case became a public sensation in 1734 becoming the single biggest newspaper story regarding England's gin craze epidemic. Judith, a young poor woman, had a two-year-old daughter, Mary. When Mary was taken away from Judith and placed into care by the local parish workhouse, Mary was provided with all new clothes.

On 29 January 1734, Judith took Mary away from the parish for a day trip and didn't return. Instead, Judith and her female accomplice "Sukey" strangled the child with a piece of linen and left the body in a ditch. Judith sold the new clothes to buy gin.

"Sir, I will tell you how I did it; but there was a Vagabond Creature, one Sukey, that persuaded me to it; and was equally concern'd with me. On Sunday Night we took the Child into the Fields, and stripp'd it, and ty'd a Linen Handkerchief hard about its Neck to keep it from crying, and then laid it in a Ditch. And after that, we went together, and sold the Coat and Stay for a Shilling, and the Petticoat and Stockings for a Groat. We parted the Money, and join'd for a Quartern of Gin."

Judith Defour's statement recorded during her trail at the Old Bailey, London, 27 February 1734.

Drink 'Til You Drop

In 1741, a group of Londoners offered a
farm labourer – who had travelled to the
big city to trade – a shilling for each pint
of gin he could sink. A proud man, the
farmer managed three pints, and then
immediately dropped down dead.*

*Gin then was 60 per cent ABV, twice as strong as it is today.

Origins No.5

When gin first became popular in
England, following the accession
of Dutch ruler William of Orange,
in 1688, a lot of the gin was first
served in pints. And flavoured
with sulphuric acid.

Make It Right No.7

Negroni

Ginventory:
- 25 ml gin
- 25 ml sweet vermouth
- 25 ml Campari
- 1 large ice cube
- 1 slice of orange to garnish
- Mixing glass

Get the Gin In:
1. Pour the gin, vermouth and Campari into a mixing glass. Add ice and stir well. Make sure the glass feels cold.
2. Strain the liquid into a tumbler.
3. Add one large ice cube.
4. Garnish with an orange slice.

Gin Wit No.15

"
Gin and drugs, dear lady, gin and drugs.
"

T. S. Eliot

Ginformation No.17

You may hear gin be classified in two forms:

"Classic Gin"

Gin that predominantly tastes of juniper,
e.g. London Dry.

Brands: Tanqueray, Beefeater, Sipsmiths,
Bombay Sapphire, Hendricks. Gordon's

"Contemporary Gin" or "New American Gin"

Gin that contain juniper but not as the main
flavour; with other botanicals taking charge –
they be from anything, ranging from lavender to
sarsaparilla. Unlike London Dry gin (which is made
from a corn base spirit), contemporary gins can be
made from rye or barley base spirit.

Brands: Nolet's Silver & Reserve, DH Krahn,
Dry Fly, Twisted Nose, Still Austin, White Mountain,
Threefold Aromatic, Fraser Valley

Know Thy Congeners

When drinkers talk of getting drunk and having hangovers, it's rarely the booze that is to blame. It's actually the biologically active chemicals in alcohol, known as congeners.

Congeners create the smell, appearance and flavour of any alcoholic drink, but they are also responsible for why in a state of brutal hangover you claim you'll never drink again.

Congeners are more active and more present in darker alcohols such as whisky, brandy and red wine. Clear spirits such as gin and vodka, have much lower levels of congeners – as much as 40 times less – and therefore give you less of an aggressive hangover. Of course, excessive drinking renders this point moot.

Gin Fingers

One of the best ways to order gin at a bar is to give the volume in terms of fingers. Or gingers, as we believe they should be called.

'Fingers' is now an arcane way of ordering gin, but if you don't have a jigger to hand a finger held up to your glass is an efficient way of pouring a single 25 ml serving. A double would be two fingers, and a triple – forbidden to be served in British pubs – is a mighty three-fingerer. Bring back fingering – or gingering! – we say.

Get Your Fix

While the word "Botanical" is a clear and present fixture on most gin bottles these days, what is less mentioned is the word "Fixative". And, without a doubt, the fixatives are the most important botanicals in a bottle of gin.

The most popular fixatives in today's gin are grains of paradise, cubeb pepper, orris root, angelica root, cassia bark and coriander seed, among scores of others.

These botanicals structurally bind the separate flavours of the gin together and give each gin brand its distinctive flavour – and they are the reason why no two gins are alike.

Gin Wit No.16

"

You'd learn more about the world by lying on the couch and drinking gin out of a bottle than by watching the news.

"

Garrison Keillor

Make It Right No.8

Gin Fizz

Ginventory:

- 2 shots of gin (70 ml)
- 1 shot of lime juice (25 ml)
- A splash of sugar syrup (1 tablespoon)
- Ice cubes
- Sparkling water
- 1 slice or wheel of lemon

Get the Gin In:
1. Pour the gin, lemon juice and sugar syrup in a cocktail shaker.
2. Fill the shaker with as many ice cubes as will fit.
3. Shake until the outside of the shaker feels cold to touch.
4. Drop large ice cubes into a highball or tall glass.
5. Strain liquid into glass over ice.
6. Top up with sparkling water.
7. Garnish with a lemon slice.

*This is also known as a Tom Collins.

CHAPTER
SIX

LET THE GIN
BE GIN

Ginformation No.18

Did you know the juniper berry – from
which all gin is made – is, in fact, not
a berry at all. It is a a highly evolved
female seed pine cone.

Gin Wit No.17

"

The only time I ever enjoyed ironing was the day I accidentally got gin in the steam iron.

"

Phyllis Diller

International
Gin & Tonic Day

If you're reading this on 19 October,
we hope you have your hands full with
a gorgeous G&T because... today... is
International Gin & Tonic Day!*

*Of course, every day is G&T day if you're a true ginthusiast.

Gin Wit No.18

"

When a man who is drinking
neat gin starts talking about his
mother he is past all argument.

"

C.S. Forester, The African Queen

Gin Wit No.19

66

For gin, in cruel sober truth,
supplies the fuel for flaming youth.

99

Noel Coward

Martini and Me No.3

Straight talking facts every true Martini lover
must know:

- The V-shaped (V is for victory!) "martini"
  glass is actually just called a cocktail glass.
  It's only been referred to as a martini glass
  in recent decades due to one becoming
  synonymous with the other.
- In 1887, the name Martini is derived from the
  city of Martinez, California.
- The slim stem of a martini glass is deliberate
  for its function. It is designed so that your
  hand would never come in touch with the bowl
  containing the cocktail (your warm hands will
  heat up and dilute the ice-cold gin)
- The wide and flat surface area of the martini
  glass creates surface tension and allows the
  bouquet of the gin to float up and tickle the
  nostrils.
- The conical shape is designed specifically to
  stop the cocktail's ingredients from separating.

The Name's Gin No.3

Ian Fleming's* fictional super spy James
Bond's famous uttering of his immortal line
"Shaken, not stirred" is perhaps the greatest
drink catchphrase of all time. And the line,
from Fleming's novels at least, refer to gin
martini's, the author's wet weapon of choice,
first appears in the fourth Bond novel,
Diamonds Are Forever (1956), though the line is
not said by Bond*.

---

* Ian Fleming loved gin. He would sometimes drink an entire
bottle a day. At his doctor's recommendation, he later switched to
bourbon as it was marginally better for his health.

* It's spoken by the third person narrator. Bond first speaks the
phrase in *Dr.No* (1958).

* Sean Connery's Bond is the first to say the line, in the third
Bond film, *Goldfinger*.

Ginformation No.19

Gin takes its name from the Dutch
word for juniper, *genever*, which in
turn is from the Old French *genevre*, an
adaptation of the Latin *juniperus*, from
which we get our word "juniper".

Gin Wit No.20

My main ambition as a gardener
is to water my orange trees
with gin, then all I have to do is
squeeze the juice into a glass.

W. C. Fields

Ginformation No.20

Gin has more affectionate nicknames than any other spirit. "Mother's Ruin," is perhaps the most adored, a moniker attributed to gin because gin was the (inexpensive) spirit of choice in whorehouses, venues that also carried out abortions. Here are just some of the other lovely names gin has been referred to throughout the course of its illustrious drinking career:

Ladies Delight
Hollands
White Satin
Partiality
Max
Royal Poverty
Dutch Courage
Tow Row
Mother's Milk
The Out And Out

South Sea Mountain
Knock Me Down
Cock My Cap
Kill Grief
The Makeshift
Blue Lightening
Cuckold's Comfort
Flashes Of Lightening
Cream Of The Valley

Gin Wit No.21

I've tried Buddhism, Scientology, numerology, Transcendental Meditation, The Kabbalah, t'ai chi, feng shui and Deepak Chopra but I find straight gin works best.

Phyllis Diller

Ginformation No.21

The juniper bush is an evergreen tree
that has soft needles instead of leaves.
It often reminds people of a Christmas
tree, and its berries do indeed have
that yuletide smell and taste to them.
It's little wonder then that British gin-
lovers spent £36m on gin in the week
before Christmas 2017.

Origins: Coriander Seeds

The second most vital ingredient for gin is coriander seeds. Just a teaspoon is required, but the seeds are the source of the spirit's flavours. The essential oil contained in the coriander seed, called linalool, produces flavours of sage, lemon and ginger and fragrant, spicy and mellow aromas.

Origins No.6

The first written use of the word "gin" appeared in *The Fable of the Bees, or Private Vices, Publick Benefits* by Bernard Mandeville, published in 1714.

The line read: "The infamous liquor, the name of which deriv'd from Juniper-Berries in Dutch, is now, by frequent use… shrunk into a monosyllable, intoxicating *Gin*.'

Let the gin begin!

Origins No.7

Juniper berries distilled in base spirit has been going on for more than a millennia. In 1055, the Benedictine Monks of Solerno in Italy, printed a recipe for "tonic wine infused with juniper berries" in their *Compendium Solernita*, a medieval textbook of sorts, as they believed it helped cure chest ailments. The juniper based wine was also employed as a remedy for poor souls who caught the Black Death, the plague. It didn't help.

Gin Wit No.22

"

A perfect Martini should be made by filling a glass with gin then waving it in the general direction of Italy.

"

Noël Coward

Martini and Me No.4

Want to sound clever the next time someone hands you a Martini at an elegant party? These quotes will help you out:

"Martinis are the only American invention as perfect as a sonnet."
H. L. Mencken

"A man must defend his home, his wife, his children and his Martini."
Jackie Gleason

"I never go jogging, it makes me spill my Martini."
George Burns

"I must get out of these wet clothes and into a dry Martini."
Mae West in Every Day's a Holiday *(1937 film)*

"I drink too much. The last time I gave a urine sample it had an olive in it."
Rodney Dangerfield

"Happiness is a dry Martini and a good woman... or a bad woman."
George Burns

"Happiness is... finding two olives in your Martini when you're hungry."
Johnny Carson

Frank Sinatra: "Let me fix you a Martini that's pure magic."

Dean Martin: "It may not make life's problems disappear, but it'll certainly reduce their size."

Gin Wit No.23

"

I exercise strong self-control. I never drink anything stronger than gin before breakfast.

"

W. C. Fields

Ginformation No.22

Scotland produces the best whisky in the world (so says us). But did you know that until 2018, 70 per cent of the UK's entire gin production was made in Scotland too?

That all changed in 2018 when England overtook Scotland for the first time, a clear sign that the gin boom was in full effect. From 2013, English distilleries boomed – tripled – from 66 to 228. In 2019, Scotland now has 186 distilleries.

The UK overall has over 450 unique gin brands, ranging from small-batch gin producers to the world's bestselling gins. The top world-leading three of which – Hendrick's, Gordon's and Tanqueray – are all made in Scotland. Why? Two reasons:

1. Scotland is abundant with juniper berries, particularly in the Highlands and moorlands.
2. Scotland's freshwater network would stretch around the world three times (more than 125,000 kilometres of rivers and streams!) as well as fresh high-quality water in more than 25,500 lochs.

Tickled Pink

The pink gin market has exploded in recent years. In 2018, only a handful of brands were making flavoured pink gin, then in 2019 the category was valued at £163 million, up a whopping 751 per cent on the same period the previous year!

Origins No.8

When the Black Death plague hit continental Europe in the mid - 1300s, doctors of that time wore face masks stuffed with crushed juniper berries and people began eating and drinking juniper water believing it would lower the risk of infection and spreading the disease. It didn't work that effectively, considering the death toll.*

*Two hundred million.

Bathtub Gin

The art of making a good gin is down to one thing: striking the right balance between the base alcoholic spirit and the use of botanicals.

When making your own compound (bathtub) gin at home, remember to think of botanicals in their most important flavouring-giving quality: essential oils.

Most of the popular botanicals employed to make gin contain essential oils, and those essential oils give gin its flavour. From juniper to coriander seeds, lemon to orange, grapefruit to angelica root, etc.

The more botanicals used to make gin, the more essential oil content, the more oil the better the gin's viscosity and texture – it's the different between a harsh alcoholic gin and a smooth gin, and a flavoursome gin and an over-flavoured or muddled gin.

Ginformation No.23

The juniper berry is a seed, not a
berry. And they are packed with
antioxidants. While they taste too
bitter to be eaten like a blueberry, a
juniper berry is medically able to
assist in fighting infection, reduce
bloating and indigestion.

Ginformation No.24

In 2013, juniper became the first species of tree to be fully collected and saved by the UK National Tree Seed project initiated by Kew's Royal Botanic Gardens, therefore ensuring gin production is safe forever, regardless of total global apocalypse. Phew!

In recent years, the juniper evergreen has been in decline due to a particular fungus decimating growth as well as deforestation. Nearly six million seeds from many tree species across the country are now stored as part of the Millennium Seed Bank.

Gin Wit No.24

"

The proper union of gin and vermouth is a great and sudden glory; it is one of the happiest marriages on earth, and one of the shortest lived.

"

Bernard DeVoto

Origins No.9

At the height of the gin craze, gin was cheap, poor quality, 80 per cent ABV, filled with harmful additives and sold by anybody who could afford to make gin. The poor would drink it to excess so much so that the death rate in 1720s London overtook the birth rate and the 500,000 population of London began to shrink for the first time since the plague half a century earlier.

More T to Your G

Simple question ... but are you bored of your G&T? Do you ever want to branch out a bit and add a little variety into your gin drinking? If so, we can highly recommend any of these tonic replacements ...

Gin and Bitter lemon

Gin and Ginger

Gin and Lime Cordial

Gin and Grapefruit

Gin and Pomegranate

Gin and Coca Cola
    (diet recommended)

Gin and Soda

Gin and Cranberry

Gin and Tomato juice
    (Red Snapper)

Gin and Soda

Gin and Irn Bru

Gin and Orange juice

Gin and Apple juice

Gin and Pineapple juice

Gin and Iced Black Tea

Gin and Strawberry juice

Gin Wit No.25

66

The Victory gin was like nitric acid, and moreover, in swallowing it one had the sensation of being hit on the back of the head with a rubber club. The next moment, however, the burning in his belly died down and the world began to look more cheerful.

99

George Orwell, 1984

* We wonder if the gin was called Victory for the V-shaped bowl of the conical cocktail glass?

Truman Capote's White Angel

In Truman Capote's *Breakfast at Tiffany's* Holly Golightly's famous drink is referred to as a White Angel by Joe Bell the barman. It's not clear if Joe called the drink White Angel because of gorgeous Golightly (played by Audrey Hepburn in the film version) or because that's actually the name of the cocktail. Anyway, the recipe as told by narrator OJ Berman is simple and it packs a wallop.

"One half vodka,
one-half gin,
no vermouth."

"Let me build you a drink. Something new. They call it a White Angel."

A Gin A Day...

Crystal clear in conscience and packed with health benefits, gin should be one of your five a day. Here's two more reasons to drink gin:

1. Juniper contains infection-fighting flavonoids plus vitamin C.
2. Juniper also includes catechins, alpha-terpineol, alpha-pinene, beman caryophyllene, limonene, menthol, rutin and delta-3-carene. (These assist with blood circulation, regulate the passing of fluids and toxins through your liver and kidneys, and aid your digestion by making your body produce more enzymes.)

Take that, medicine!

Gin Wit No.26

"

The most dangerous drink is gin. You have to be really, really careful with that. And you also have to be 45, female and sitting on the stairs. Because gin isn't really a drink, it's more a mascara thinner. 'Nobody likes my shoes!' 'I made... I made fifty... fucking vol-au-vents, and not one of you... not one of you... said "Thank you."' And my favourite: 'Everybody, shut up. Shut up! This song is all about me.'

"

Dylan Moran

Ginformation No.25

Drinking gin is getting more expensive!

In the UK, a 700 ml bottle of gin costs an average of £23.06, compared with £18.91 five years ago. Its most common mixer, tonic water, is also up 18 per cent over the same period. Whose to blame? Millennials, of course.

Those born between 1981 and 1996 are driving the growth of the premium gin market thanks to the emotive and skilled use of social media by distilleries and bars. Today, in London, a G&T costs an average of £8.82, one of the worst offenders for inflated prices in the world.

The average cost of a G&T across all countries now stands at £9.25.